"In physics, when a wave is 90 degrees out of phase it is invisible or imperceptible; these phases, in terms of subtle personality facets, can be positive or negative. The best thing about Laura Hansen's 'wrench' is that it twists the phases into the light of love, spiritual awareness, and well-being. And, by the way, the wrench she uses and teaches you to use is also the light of love! Laura is a great teacher and counselor, and a blessing to anyone who crosses her path..."

R. L. Amoroso
Director, Noetic Advanced Studies Institute
Author of over 30 books on consciousness

"Laura will take you on a journey of self-discovery in a way that is fun, powerful, and inspiring. Read this book. It will help you make sense of every part of your life."

Karen Russo
Award-winning author of
The Money Keys: Bringing Peace, Freedom and Real Financial Power

"*Hand me a Wrench, My Life Is Out of Whack* will enable you to discover that underneath the exterior of your mortal self lies true happiness and strength. I highly recommend this book to anyone who wants to move past the blocks that are stopping them from achieving their fullest potential."

Teresa Anne Power
Author of the award-winning *The ABCs of Yoga for Kids*

"Finally a personal development book that says it like it is, in a fun and intimate way. *Hand Me a Wrench, My Life Is Out of Whack* allows us to look at our infinite potential in a very unique light."

Mario P. Cloutier
President, Shopper Marketer

"Laura is one of those rare individuals you cannot forget. Her insight, compassion, and understanding of the lives we lead make her a valuable guide and teacher. I have known and worked with Laura for over 20 years. She is someone worth knowing and this experience will change your life."

M. Kay Robinson
InSight Intuitive Consulting
Board Member, National Association of Women Business Owners
San Francisco Chapter

"Laura helped me heal issues that stemmed from my earliest childhood memories. She inspired me to let go of the story that had been running me for years and helped me to embrace the healing that was always there for me. Every time we talk I sense she is watching without judgment, guiding me to open my eyes even wider so I don't miss out on all the good parts."

Mitch Newman
www.TheRelationshipCoach.com

"*Hand Me a Wrench, My Life Is Out of Whack* is a wonderful book for everyone who thinks life is more complicated than it needs to be. Laura Hansen is a special soul who has a unique gift in helping people shift life experiences and patterns and making them easier to break through. Her direct, playful way of illustrating challenging situations makes this a must-read for anyone who is in the midst of a life overhaul or just needs of little soul (spring) cleaning!"

Nina Boski
LifeBites Media

"As a teacher, Laura offers a unique blend of wit, intelligence, compassion, and side-splitting humor. Her laser-like insight coupled with a great sense of play and amusement make her undeniably a voice worth listening to."

Lynne Webb
Founder, Soul Tree Adventures

"'GIFTED' doesn't even begin to describe Laura Hansen's abilities. She is truly a remarkable healer and teacher. As an entrepreneur, I have been blessed with Laura's tools and exercises to navigate the complexities, anxieties, and growing pains of a new business. Working with Laura has been transformational – giving me a greater sense of clarity, ease, and business growth!"

Leah Burdick
Partner, www.TheVisionaryAgency.com

"Funny, wise, and uplifting! Laura Hansen's delightful personality and humor are captured in her book and its down-to-earth and practical metaphors. I had so much fun reading it and laughing out loud, I finished it in one sitting. Now I look forward to going back and doing the exercises. Her fun and encouraging prose offers a lighter and hopeful catalyst for change. I plan on ordering a bunch of books and offering them to my clients. Besides…you gotta love the title!"

Susan Rueppel, Ph.D.
Business Intuitive, www.energeticwisdom.com

(Continued on page 111)

Kathy—

Hand Me a Wrench,
My Life Is Out of Whack

To your beautiful life.

xo Laura

*An Introduction to **Life Mechanics**™*

Hand Me a Wrench, My Life Is Out of Whack

Understanding the Decisions We Make and Discovering the Power to Change

Laura Hansen

TAYLOR HILL PRESS

Published by:

TAYLOR HILL PRESS

Taylor Hill Press
P.O. Box 582952
Elk Grove, CA 95758
916-596-3016
info@taylorhillpress.com
www.taylorhillpress.com

The information contained in this book offers techniques and tools for personal wellness and growth. It can be used in conjunction with, but is not a substitute for, appropriate or necessary professional medical or psychological care. Discussing any new approaches you are introducing into your life with your trusted healthcare professional will benefit you and the attainment of your goals.

Publisher's Cataloging-In-Publication Data

Hansen, Laura.

    Hand me a wrench, my life is out of whack : an introduction to Life Mechanics : understanding the decisions we make and discovering the power to change / Laura Hansen.

    p. : ill. ; cm.

    ISBN: 978-0-9841953-0-5

1. Self-actualization (Psychology) 2. Decision making. 3. Love. 4. Interpersonal relations. 5. Conduct of life. I. Title.

BF637.S4 H36 2010

158.1   2009934694

Printed in the United States of America on acid-free paper.
15 14 13 12 11   2 3 4 5 6

Cover Designer: Lubosh Cech of Oko Design Studio, www.okodesignstudio.com

Book Designer: Peri Poloni-Gabriel of Knockout Design, www.knockoutbooks.com

Author Photographer: Cheryl Savan, www.savanphoto.com

Illustrator: Joy Reid

Book Producer: Brookes Nohlgren, www.booksbybrookes.com

To anyone who has said to themselves,

"There's got to be more to my life than this."

Contents

Introduction

This is a compassionate, roll-up-your-sleeves, find-out-what's going-on kind of book. It's not about "think good thoughts and good things will happen." It is quite specific in helping you understand the mechanics of your life – the what, how, and why of your life experiences – so that you can truly make your life your own.

As we seek to understand our lives, and how to live them meaningfully, we begin to realize something: the days of believing we are broken, and need to be fixed by someone or something else, are coming to an end. We are ready to consider, as a culture, that all individuals have inherent value, free will, a valid point of view, and an infinite capacity to understand, change, and command their own life.

Of the many discussions taking place in our society, there are two conversations I find particularly exciting. One is the discussion around the importance of making conscious choices. This is a good discussion to have. Most everyone agrees that conscious choices are better than choices we make without thinking or by repeating the same behavior.

The other conversation, a whispering really, is among the new, young scientists who believe we aren't just complex biological life forms – that we contain something more: a vital aspect of us that is not entirely material, not entirely measurable. This quiet revolution will bring fresh ideas to the scientific discussion of consciousness, about what "conscious" really means, if it exists – and, if it does, how it works.

While these two discussions, along with many others, slowly shift the nation's consciousness, a growing social phenomenon will speed things along – individuals are exploring the capacity of their own consciousness. They're not waiting for the next great solution to their problems. Or, for science to prove or disprove that consciousness exists. And, they're not waiting for traditional religions to admit that direct communication between a person and their God is a natural, everyday occurrence.

According to recent polls, nearly 90% of Americans believe there is a soul. Over half the country has left religion in favor of exploring the concept and practice of their own spirituality. A growing number have found various forms of meditation to bring a calm and an insight that have been missing in their lives. And, more and more people are saying, "I don't need someone telling me what's wrong with me. I want to understand how my life works. I'll take it from there, thank you very much."

What will come to pass, as we collectively understand how our lives work, is a meaningful and positive shift in how we think, love, work, and create community.

I'm among the 50% who went looking for what made them tick. Shortly after college, I entered an intensive human development training program. Going in, my main questions were the questions most of us have: "Who am I?" "Why am I here?" "What is my purpose?" "How can I live the life I envision?" "Why is change so difficult even though I wish to change?" "Why is my life so challenging?" During my over 20 years, first as a student, then as a teacher, I found my answers to those questions as well as many more, and have shown others how to find their own answers to these same questions. Note: not give them *my* answers (my answers won't work for anyone else), rather the tools for finding their own.

The first step of Life Mechanics is understanding – and experiencing – the strength we have to shape our lives. From this foundation of inner stability, many more things are possible. And, we can, in our daily lives, be equipped to stop ourselves and say, "Aha! Wait! Let me do this differently."

Whatever your beliefs about yourself are, I guarantee you that nobody – nobody – is more committed to your growth than you. This is a fundamental truth of your consciousness. The job of this book is to give you a fun, powerful way to unlock and use this truth for yourself.

Happiness is breaking all the rules.

I guarantee that all the rules you follow in your life that lead to "Wow, why do I keep doing that?" and "Ugh, I didn't do myself any good there, did I?" didn't flow from the joy in your heart. They may have come from your family, your religion, your culture, the media, or your friends.

Breaking these rules doesn't mean you can't love and respect those who have guided you in your life. It only means you're getting rid of what doesn't work for you. It's just common sense – your own unique brand of common sense. A type of common sense that may not make sense to anyone else.

Yes, I know we're talking crazy here, but if you're going to give freedom and happiness a chance, you must understand the difference between your love for family, tradition, peers, and teachers from the love you have for yourself. At some point in the future, the people who truly wish the best for you will support your new lifestyle. They may even join you. It's very possible that they don't like the rules they live by either.

No doubt you have tried to make these rules work, wondering what's wrong with you. Nothing's wrong with you. You may have spent more time figuring out what's wrong with you than you've spent recognizing what's right with you. It's the rules you're using that clearly don't apply.

Rules that lead to questions such as…

+ *Is it okay to respect yourself if your dad doesn't respect you?*

+ *Is it okay to enjoy the fresh smell of the air after a rain when you are unemployed?*

+ *Just how much joy should you let yourself have if you still have problems and unfulfilled goals?*

I'm sure each of us has a crime/punishment chart displayed in our psyche somewhere. We've gotten pretty good at punishing ourselves – at sentencing ourselves for our mistakes and inadequacies. When I was a kid, I would leave a sign on my bedroom door that stated my crime (broke lamp/spilled juice/locked sister out of house) and the length of time I would stay in my room plus the number of meals I would miss. It sounds quaint and funny now, but old habits die hard. To this day, I still catch myself referring to my own crime/punishment chart. *Crime: Failed to complete an unrealistic number of things in one day. Punishment: Eat 12 corn chips and one slice of cheese for dinner.* I just shake my head, laugh, and make a real dinner … most of the time.

Our reason for doing this is a good one. We wish to be good people. We wish to make other people happy. We wish to learn and grow.

We wish to show respect for ourselves and for each other so we can build strong families and communities.

However, this method doesn't work. We end up limiting our choices by how worthy we think we are of them. "I'd love to take a day off to go skiing, but I was impatient with my son last week. I'll work late instead." Or, "My co-worker told a funny joke, but I'm not going to laugh because he didn't get his report to me on time. I'll show him."

We make these crazy decisions all day long. We purposely rob ourselves of laughter, playfulness, happiness, and wealth. It's madness. Have you ever consciously decided not to hug someone you loved because he or she made you mad earlier that day? You chose to deprive yourself of one of your favorite activities as their punishment? With your one simple decision, you made yourself sad, eroded the foundation of your relationship a little bit, and made him or her feel guilty. What a success that was!

To change why we make these types of life decisions, we need to adopt a different method for being a good person and making good decisions. A method based upon our nature of love, acceptance, and integrity. I know, this is easier said than done. Humor me. Let's just say it's possible. And, if it is possible, how do we get from here to there?

You can change anything.

Everything in your life is find-able, definable, and changeable. Not just in the abstract, but also in the activity of your everyday life: You can figure it out. You can change how you think about yourself. You can find the source of the parts of your life that don't work. And, you can make decisions that free you instead of trap you. There is nothing in your life that you can't find and change.

But, who is the YOU that you are freeing? If you have thought yourself not a very good person, or not a very valuable person, then recognizing the difference between you and the judgmental view you have of yourself may be tricky.

Therefore, the first step is to consider that if you dig down under everything in your life, you will find that you are good and that you have value. As an introduction to Life Mechanics, this book will help you take steps in recognizing the beauty of who you are, the core motivations for your decisions, and how to make new decisions that reflect the happiness and strength within you.

At the end of every chapter there is an exercise or technique that directly relates to the chapter topic. I've included these activities as a way for you to immediately take steps toward understanding your life and making new decisions.

In the tens of thousands of people I've worked with over the years, most everyone knew EXACTLY what changes they needed to make and how they wished to live their lives. That was the easy part. The difficultly was accepting that they were worth changing for.

And that is why I am writing this book to you. Really, it's a love poem about your beauty, strength, and joy. It's also a call to action for you to be an activist for your own life. For you to be the strongest advocate on your behalf, lobbying with yourself every moment to make the choice that best serves you, builds your life, and brings you happiness.

I should warn you that this is a love poem with unconventional imagery. You will find in this book that I talk about life, the soul, and free will in terms of ice cream, table decorations, store shelves, baking, and other everyday things. I do this because our lives are everyday things. We don't need to ascend to a higher consciousness to understand the meaning of our lives. We can find the meaning right here – in our lives – where we live.

*This is **your life**.*

*You have the **vision** and*

*the **power** to live it*

your way.

One

You're good…
You're "ice cream" good.

Barely out the door of the ice cream parlor, I took the first lick of my pistachio ice cream cone. Then, the giant scoop fell on the ground. I stared at it for a second, deciding whether I should pick it up or not. I really, really wanted that ice cream. I did pick it up, and I pushed it back in the cone. Next, with my fingers, I carefully removed the bits of gravel and other stuff from the side that touched the sidewalk. Happy enough with my work, off I went with my ice cream cone.

I made two decisions that dramatically changed my experience that day. First, I decided that the ice cream scoop was worth saving. Second, I wanted to enjoy my ice cream as much as possible, so I took a few minutes to remove the stuff that had gotten stuck in it from its fall to the ground.

My experience of eating the ice cream would have been very different had I not first removed the debris. It could have been one of the grossest eating experiences of my life if I ate it gravel and all. Quite possibly, I would have stopped eating ice cream altogether because of the inevitable taste bud flashbacks.

I tell you this story because all of us know the difference between the ice cream and the pavement junk. But, we may have difficulty telling the difference when it comes to ourselves. To be clear, in the above story, you are the ice cream – not the bugs, gravel, and dog hair sticking to it.

Your creamy goodness is in there, under it all. Sometimes, you get a glimpse of it. If you forget that you are the ice cream, you don't think you can dust yourself off after a fall. And, even if you do remember you are good, you may not believe you have the strength or the right to repair your life and move on.

That's why there are parts of your life that you don't like licking, so to speak. You start dreading going to work, or coming home to your roommate, or looking at yourself in the mirror. When you think you can't or shouldn't forgive yourself every time you pick your life up off the pavement, then pretty soon you can't taste the original flavor of your life at all. You begin believing that you are not good, and that you don't have what it takes to make your life better.

Have you ever been daydreaming, or maybe walking through nature, when you have a flash of clarity about your life? Then, before you know it, the usual thoughts about financial problems, relationship issues, and personal difficulties come crowding back in? Well, in that flash, you remembered how to live according to your nature. That's good! That's you saying to yourself, "Hey, I'm the good part! All the rest can be removed."

Your inherent goodness – your ice-creaminess – is absolute and permanent.

You are good because *you are a soul*. You are a soul living a physical life, but a soul nonetheless. Souls are embodiments of the eternal consciousness present in all life. The soul, the eternal self, is connected to and is part of the grace and love of this eternal consciousness. This essence is acknowledged in all spiritual faiths and practices. In this book, I'll be using the term "God" to represent this cosmic consciousness.

Though you may be making choices that lead to difficult life experiences, you remain the soul that you were, are, and always will be. You are always the ice cream. Although your life may taste like ice cream that's fallen in a landfill, there's nothing wrong with you, the soul. But, clearly some ice cream surgery is necessary. And, in the meantime, you've got to watch where you're licking.

Perhaps you've asked, "How can I improve myself?" How can you overcome your addictions, bad habits, dysfunctions, failures, personality defects, childhood issues, and so on? From the point of view of you as an eternal soul, you don't have to overcome anything. You are already stronger than all of your issues combined. You allow your problems to color your self-image because you believe that the core of you is defined by your actions.

The truth about your goodness is the other way around: The core of you (your soul) shines through the ideas you have about yourself and how life is supposed to be. Just as the sun shines through a stained glass window to cast colored light through a room, so does your soul shine through your life to cast light tinted by your thoughts. Your thoughts color the glass, but the sun that is you remains bright and clear. Remembering this fact is vital to your finding the enthusiasm to change the color of the glass to one that pleases you. Just because a thought is running through your mind doesn't mean you must pay attention to it. Not all thoughts are worth your time and effort.

For example, let's say you would like to get rid of a habit or a fear. What will take its place after you remove it? Until you find something better to replace it, you won't let it go. If you don't believe that *you* are that something better, then you will keep the problem or try to mask it with a more socially acceptable behavior. That's why developing goals and plans is important for your happiness. Doing so helps you direct your attention to what you wish to do instead of what you feel you're stuck with. However, first you've got to remember that you are the good part, and that everything else is removable.

If you can't find the trigger to remembering your true self – the experience that will remind you that you are soulful creamy goodness – you might replace the current problem with a more socially accept-able, but still unhealthy, behavior. The new mask may make everyone around you happy, but it will fall short nonetheless. Because you desire acceptance from others, you'll try it, but the replacement will only leave you feeling empty.

An example would be that you quit smoking, but now you overeat. Or, if you can't manage your anger, you exercise four hours a day as an outlet. You haven't found and removed the source of the behavior, but you've dealt with the symptom in a way that is acceptable to others.

Those acceptable but inadequate replacements can take you to a place of quiet despair. They're just band-aids. You still haven't made a connec-tion, which is what you're longing for. You still haven't remembered that you are inherently good. Instead, you believe that there is no good place within you for making better decisions. At this point, you've completely forgotten you are ice cream. Now, you're just licking the pavement!

Having faith in a higher power can be a path to remembering that you are a soul. God is communicating with you all day long – through gentle whispers, a soft breeze on your face, a quiet moment in the sun – but if you're so wrapped up in the issues of your life, you won't listen – God's voice just sounds annoying and ridiculously cheerful, so you ignore it. Sometimes you can find that soul-to-soul connection from someone else – from the soul within me to the soul within you. Or you might find your memory of who you are as you walk in nature, feel the sea breeze, or breathe the mountain air. Your soul never stops calling to you.

Remember, you are good and unscathed by the events and decisions of your life. Your soul endures and is with you through it all. Your soul *is* you. Everything else is stuff in your ice cream... Everything else is colored glass.

You are not your mistakes.
You are not the product of the life you live.

You created your life through your choices, but you are a creative force separate from your life – separate from your choices. You are not your personality of weird behaviors and quirks. You are not the person others kindly or harshly declare you to be.

The stunning glow within the checkout clerk... the sunny beam of joy coming from the man sifting through the dumpster... the soft light behind the critical eyes of the executive hailing a cab. Regardless of the lives they lead, the radiance of their souls shines through. They may not see it or believe that it exists as anything more than a dream, but it's there, real and alive.

Have you ever noticed this in the people around you? That in spite of how a person was expressing himself, you saw his beauty within? Maybe you felt loving warmth when he walked in the room. Did you walk away from the conversation lighter? Did you realize that you witnessed something special, but couldn't put your finger on it? These are moments when you saw the soul shine through.

Seeing the soul shine through in daily life.

Several years ago, while I was having lunch with a colleague, a simple but extraordinary thing happened. We didn't know each other very well. We were working on a project together, so we got together for lunch to discuss it. After the meeting, I drove him to his home office and parked in front of his house.

We were both standing outside the car with the car doors open, chatting over the car's roof. At the end of the conversation, before turning to go, he made one last remark. His voice took on a quiet clarity. The traffic noise disappeared. The sound of the birds and wind fell away to silence. The only thing in the world I could hear was the voice of my work-mate floating through the air like musical notes, "You're doing a very good job, Laura. You'll be fine." My work-mate was a bit of a tough guy who never made these types of remarks. Even then, I knew God was present with us talking through him. That instant would create a shock wave through my life and my future.

Then, just as quickly as it had come, the moment was gone. The world's noise started again, and everything was back to normal. My friend was saying good-bye and patting the car hood with the palm of his hand. I don't believe he had any memory of what he had just said. From that day, he made no such similar comment or ever referenced what he had said.

From that experience, I knew I had a chance of finding my life again. If I could have this experience once, I could have it again. Maybe I'm not so bad a person after all. It would take me many years to embrace as true what I am about to tell you.

Your soul is not damaged by thoughts, or experience. Your soul remains clear and bright. Over time, however, your thoughts, the thoughts of others, emotional pain, and fears surround it – making your shining soul difficult for you to see or remember. You find yourself licking the fallen ice cream scoop without brushing it off first. By then, all you can taste is the gravelly bits. Enjoying the taste of the ice cream in between is not really possible.

When we get to this point, we lose our joy. We get discouraged. We resign ourselves to a life of icky licks with maybe a random tasty bite now and then. So, we compromise, follow orders, do what everyone else does, and try to dull the pain. But, what we really wish for is the life we dream of living.

The goal of this chapter is to get to a place where you can consider the reality that you are still a good scoop of ice cream. The hard work isn't letting go of the fears and insecurities within you that have developed over the years. The hard work is accepting the reality that you are good, that you are the soul. Once you do that, restoring your life is possible and much simpler than you might think.

The task at hand is remembering your true self.

You can distinguish between you (the soul) and the details of your life. When you do, you will find that the difference is as stark as it is between you and the car you drive, or you and the clothes you wear, or ice cream and pavement.

This task can be very difficult, though. Sometimes you walk through your day in a constant state of fear that you will make another mistake or that people can tell that you don't know what you're doing. That's when you fantasize about staying in bed under the covers. During these times, you are identifying yourself with your past actions and your mistakes. You can step out of this frame of mind by giving yourself a few minutes in the morning, or at any point during the day, to write out how you'd like the day to go and how you wish to feel about yourself throughout the day.

I know that what I am suggesting sounds simple. Yet what you are doing is actually huge. You are recognizing yourself as separate from your past and in control of your life. You are saying, "I am making a new choice about my life today. If I don't, then the choices I've already made and the self-image I already have will steer my thoughts and actions."

Have you ever thrown away a beautiful dish because it was dirty? Probably not. More than likely, you washed the dish because you knew that its original condition didn't include smears of peanut butter. The problem most of us have is that we have forgotten our original condition. We don't know to release the residue that collects in us from an experience or from someone else's thought about who we are. We've been walking around with peanut butter on us for so long that we assume it is part of us. To make things worse, other people assume that we made a conscious decision to keep the peanut butter, so they include it in their view of us.

So, here you are: a beautiful, capable, amazing soul slowly losing the memory of yourself – too many strong emotions and judgments drowning out your real voice. Your brother's jealousy, your mother's self-loathing, your girlfriend's fear, heartbreak from your first love. Unless you find a way to remember that you are eternal and separate from your life, you will go through life repeating the frustrating experiences.

You, the soul, are not a fantasy or a heartfelt wish. Your eternal soul can be seen, felt, and heard every moment of every day. Your eternal soul is not a faint wisp of feathery air. The force of your soul shapes your life. From the moment of your birth to your last breath, your thoughts affect the lives of every person in the world.

Every thought you think reinforces itself within you and within those around you. We are indeed connected and influence each other. When you laugh, others are freer to laugh. When you are sad, those around you empathize. Because of our fundamental connection as souls, the joy one feels is transmitted globally. Just as we have come to understand the global effects of weather patterns, so are we all affected by each other's weather – the expression of our souls in our daily lives.

Your soul has the power to transform your life with a single thought.

With a simple word or phrase, you can change minds, fill hearts, lift pain, and bring joy. No other force in the world has more power to transform than your one thought. You see evidence of this every day in your own life. Whatever thought you have determines your mood, influences your decisions, and colors your perspective of the world.

Each instance in your life is an opportunity to remember that you are an eternal soul living a physical life. You are the clear, passionate force learning to know itself. Your life is a tool for you to learn how to be more you. On some level, everything you've encountered in your life has been an opportunity for you to acknowledge the difference between the ice cream and the pavement: self-love or cruelty, joy or fear, compassion or rage, wellness or depletion. We have the opportunity to discover our true selves, time and time again.

Have you ever wondered why you keep repeating the same type of experience? Each time a slightly different version of the same theme? What you are doing is choosing to recreate the experience or scenario until you do it *your* way – like perfecting a recipe. "Hmmm, that wasn't quite what I wanted. Too much of my parents' judgment... Not quite enough creativity... Just the right amount of confidence. Okay, let's do it again."

That's why taking time after an experience to understand your behavior and honor your actions is so beneficial to your happiness and growth. If you don't compassionately evaluate what you put in the mixing bowl, then you can't adjust the recipe for the next batch. You'll just make another bad cake.

And, it's easy to make a bad cake in our society. All day long we are judged by how we live. We are identified by what our lives look like. Classified by them. Passed up, eliminated, crossed off, ignored, misunderstood, or praised, promoted, celebrated. No matter which way the judgment falls, it always lands in the cake batter.

I don't care what kind of life you live; I'm only interested in your recognizing that you shine through it. That you remember – if only for an instant – that you exist as that creamy goodness, now and in every moment to come. That you are free to remember that you are a soul.

The harsh judgments you've accepted about who you are often override your soul's ability to choose well. You believe that a better choice is not available to you because you don't have the character to choose it. That there's no good part left that can make a good choice. This belief is a choice, not the absolute truth. You can make a new choice. You can lift your eyes from the pavement and look up.

You are right here, right now, shining like the sun.

You may have chosen to focus on the spot on the sidewalk instead of the clear rays of the sun, but only your point of view has changed, not you. Your soul is the incorruptible part of you – an unchangeable essence inspiring the best thoughts and actions in your life. It holds the compassion you feel, or hope to feel, for your life and for others. Its strength can spread the peace that you know is possible in the world. If you wish, you can choose to shape your life. Doing so requires letting go of the concept that you are not truly good, or that happiness is not possible.

So, pick the stuff out of the ice cream, wash the dish, choose a different color glass, bake a new cake, or whatever… I've got more metaphors if you need them!

Tips to getting the most benefit from the chapter exercises.

Following are some suggestions for making the most of the exercises you'll find at the end of each chapter. After teaching tens of thousands of people, I can tell you that most everyone pushes themselves too hard, to do too much, too fast, to get it perfectly right. The rest stare at the page paralyzed in doubt and fear. That's why I'm giving you these guidelines. They will help you foster a more compassionate self-reflection process – with possibly a smile on your face. So, please take your time and enjoy yourself. Every exercise you do, you do because you love yourself.

1. *This is YOUR book. You don't have to do any of the exercises if you don't wish to!*

2. *You are doing this for you, not to solve a problem someone else believes you have.*

3. *Do them at your own pace: whether you do them all in one sitting, or complete one a year, do them at a pace that is comfortable to you. If you find that halfway through an exercise you wish to take a break, take one – stretch, have a snack, take a bath, pet the dog...*

4. *Have snacks, your favorite beverage, music, and anything else on hand. Create a nice environment for yourself. These exercises are about your life, so you might as well celebrate your life now and the life you are building by treating yourself well.*

5. *If you find ways to address the same questions using a different medium, go for it. Almost all of these exercises are presented as a Question/Answer format. In several chapters, I suggest art-based approaches as well. For example, if you discover that*

you would rather express your thoughts and find insight through painting or collage, do it. The important part is your exploration of the questions so that you can get your answers.

Chapter 1 Exercise

This exercise can be done with paper and a pen/pencil. If you are the kind of person who likes to work with your hands, you can add a project with Play-doh, clay, mashed potatoes, or ice cream – any substance you can mold into a ball or mound that can hold little objects like paperclips, pebbles, and so on.

Step 1:

Use a letter-size paper or larger. Draw a line down the center of both sides of the paper to divide it into four vertical sections.

Starting from the left, title the four columns:

1. *Ice Cream*

2. *Pavement*

3. *Source*

4. *Strength*

In the "Ice Cream" column, write down all of the characteristics you love about yourself. Also write down the type of person you'd like to be that you're not already. Be honest with yourself. This exercise is a private activity. You don't have to show it to anyone, so go for it and don't hold back.

In the "Pavement" column, write down all of the characteristics, habits, fears, and weaknesses that make your life difficult and make you feel bad about yourself.

You can add your "Working with your hands" project here...
(Use a material that can be formed into a firm mound. For each "Other" item, add a pebble, paperclip, etc., to your mound.)

Step 2:

In Column 3, titled "Source," write down the source of each item. For example:

> Column 2: **Pavement:** If you wrote: *"Afraid I won't be successful"*

> Column 3: **Source:** *Parents always told me that I wouldn't amount to anything.*

When you write down the sources of the items on your list, just go with the first thing you think of. That's usually correct. What you're doing is giving yourself the answer before any other thought tries to cover up the truth.

Step 3:

Notice that you know the source of the judgments and fears that distract you from enjoying your life. You just had to take a few minutes to talk to yourself.

Step 4:

In Column 4, titled "Strength," ask yourself, "What is the strength that the Column 3 statement devalues?" For example:

> **Pavement:** *"Afraid I won't be successful"*

> **Source:** *Parents always told me that I wouldn't amount to anything.*

> **Strength:** *My ability to do anything I set my mind to.*

Write this **Strength** in the fourth column.

As you write the Strength for each, cross a line through the Column 2 ("Pavement") statement that corresponds to it. In the end, all you should have is a list of strengths you have restored by plucking the "debris" statements out of your life.

"Working with your hands" project here...
(As you cross off an item, remove one piece of stuff from your mound until you just have the mound – no stuff in it. When all the stuff is out, smooth your mound so it looks nice.)

If you have any items you just couldn't bring yourself to cross off, that's okay. Over the next few days, you will start to observe this particular behavior in a new way. You will get insight and the answers you are looking for. Then, you can go back and cross it off your list.

Step 5:

On a separate sheet of paper, write down 1) what decisions and changes you'll make that shine through your strengths. Also write down 2) the types of decisions you will no longer be making because they reinforce other people's ideas.

For example, you may decide 1) to begin walking with your head up and smiling and 2) to stop hanging out with people who are self-destructive.

Step 6:

Be especially patient with yourself in the coming days, weeks, and month. Remember, you are changing years' worth of behavior and decision-making. Acknowledge every successful step, no matter how small. Your life is worth celebrating.

*You are **not sin**;*

*you are **original love**.*

*You are **not small**;*

*you are **limitless**.*

Two | You do it all for LOVE.

Every good choice and every bad choice you've ever made, you've made for love.

Have you ever changed your personality a little (or a lot) depending upon who you were talking to? Or maybe suppressed your ideas because that person would judge you? You desire that person to accept you, so you twist yourself into an acceptable shape. Your decision may compromise your own joy, but at least you have a relationship now. You did what you did for whatever measure of love that person could give you.

When I use the word "love," I'm referring to the nature of our souls that seeks a relationship of acknowledgement, acceptance, communication, and creativity with all life. If the soul cannot find a way to forge a relationship with these qualities, it will come as close as it can.

If we see no other choices, we'll often compromise our own journey. Even if the relationship is damaging everyone involved, we'll slow down, speed up, or go off course to stay connected. Our desire to have communion with each other is very strong. Difficult relationships, yard work, dysfunctional work environments, boring movies, screaming fights, lying in the sun, laughing with friends… all of it, we do for love.

Understanding how strongly your desire for love and acceptance motivates your decisions can help you make choices that serve you. When you accept yourself and your thoughts, those around you are more accepting of you too. And, when you choose expression instead of suppression of your thoughts, you experience the love within you – the love that you are. In that moment, you free yourself from judgment and from the control of others. Joy replaces your desperation. Enthusiasm replaces your fear. You have chosen to shine through clear glass.

But, when you forget that you are a soul whose essence is love, you feel something is missing from your life. You look for someone to bring love to you. You beg them to fill the spot where your memory of your love for yourself belongs. In these situations, other agendas can arise. The other person may realize that they can manipulate your actions and thoughts by promising and then withholding their love. You do whatever they ask and think whatever they wish you to think, with the hope of filling your emptiness with their love. But that love will never come. The love will never come because the other person has no love to give. Like you, they have lost their memory of the love within them. The difference is that they are no longer seeking love; they have chosen to seek pain. All they have is the loss. Thus, loss is all they have to give.

In your life, do you have relationships that exhibit some of the characteristics above? Which relationships are based upon trust and acceptance? The level of miscommunication and anxiety in a relationship is directly related to how much freedom you give each other to express who you really are.

Love and the tacky centerpiece.

In many of your important relationships, both of you may wish to make the relationship work, but things get in the way. Think of it this way: Have you ever tried to have a conversation with someone at a loud dinner table – people leaning in and out of your line of sight, tall centerpieces obstructing your view? You can't hear all of the other person's words. You lose sight of the expression on their face. It's not a good experience. When this happens, do you blame yourself or the other person for the situation? Of course not. It's obvious to both of you that there are just things in the way, so you simply decide to go outside to talk, away from the distractions.

The choreography between us as souls is similar. Your judgments, fears, memories, joys, and heartbreak behave like physical objects obstructing your view, blocking eye contact and muffling words. As a soul you are fine, but those things getting in your way creates the problems.

When you remember that you can leave the noisy dinner table, so to speak, you can enjoy a quieter, uninterrupted relationship (the exercise at the end of this chapter will help jog your memory). But, when you forget that you have the power to move obstacles aside, to move the conversation to a better place, you believe that your only choice is to let the obstacles impair your communication, resulting in needlessly frustrating, unfulfilling exchanges.

Yet you continue to endure it all for love – for those moments when you catch the sparkle in each other's eye, or enjoy the quiet lull in the surrounding noise. But you don't have to settle for this. You have the power to slide the tacky centerpiece out of the way, or move the conversation to the quiet grass and create a conversation soul to soul. For the light of the soul within you or within another can only be seen through the clear glass of acceptance, with all colors of judgment removed. As you do this next exercise, you may find that you understand your relationships more than you think you do and have a pretty good idea of how you'd like to change them.

Chapter 2 Exercise

Soul-to-soul conversation.

The following exercise is one method for identifying what you'd like to move out of the way so you can have great relationships. This type of conversation is simple, but it can feel like work because you are actively changing your behavior while you are talking and listening.

You can move through these questions quickly, maybe taking 10 minutes to answer all of them. Then, you can go back through, adding depth to your answers. You may find this a more effective method than moving slowly and contemplatively through each question initially.

And, it may take several conversations with the other person to get all the way through the questions you'll ask yourself. Or you may just sit down with a pad and paper and answer these questions about a specific relationship you'd like to improve:

I'd like a better relationship with _____

If you wish, find two objects that represent you and the other person: salt and pepper shakers, stuffed animals, sea shells, etc. Doing so will give you a measure of emotional distance, putting you in a lighter, more forgiving frame of mind. Plus, it's kinda fun.

1. *During a conversation, how do I feel around them?*

2. *What emotions are stimulated within me?*

3. *What judgments do I have about myself?*

4. *How do I compare myself to this person?*

5. What are my judgments about the other person?

6. What list of expectations do I compare this person's behavior against?

7. What past hurts and mistakes affect either of our abilities to express ourselves freely?

8. What is the purpose of the relationship?

9. What foundation have the two of us built for it?

10. What kind of relationship would I like to have with this person?

11. Do I think the kind of relationship I desire is possible with this person? Can they commit to making some changes?

12. Am I willing to make changes even if they don't?

When you answer these questions honestly, you will know where the tacky centerpieces are, and where you'd like to move the conversation. You may find other questions that are appropriate to address. You may also find that answering these questions takes time and reflection. Whatever it takes, that's okay.

You may wish to share your exploration with the other person, if you feel safe enough to do that. Understanding the dynamics of your relationship with this person will give you the information you need to make new decisions.

You may, however, discover that this relationship is not worth saving. That's okay, too. Sometimes this happens. You can still appreciate and love this person for who they are. Not all of us are prepared or suited to engage with everyone else. After all, not all great flavors of ice cream taste great together.

When you stand in the **beauty**
of who **you are**,
the sky **opens**.
The **earth** rests under your **feet**.
The sun **shines**.
The **breeze** carries your **song**
across the **world**.

Three

You can go anywhere, so spread out the map.

Deep in the wilderness, a man stands in the snow surveying the landscape around him. He knows where he wishes to be, and this isn't it. He begins to hike out. For miles through treacherous terrain, fighting off predators and disoriented by blizzards, he keeps his course. Weeks later, he arrives at a quiet little town. Gasping, ragged, wild-eyed, and triumphant he pushes open the doors of the café. Everyone turns to look, thinking, "Boy, that guy must have really wanted to get here. I just rolled out of bed and walked a block. Looks like he started three states over. Get this man a cup of coffee."

We all start in different places. Like the man in the wilderness, sometimes it's far from the place we wish to be. Where we start has nothing to do with our value as people. Starting in the slums has as much value as starting in a mansion. However, to what degree we value ourselves separate from our starting point determines how much of our lives – and the world – we can explore.

Many of us lament our beginning: our childhood, our social standing, and our hardships. If we value ourselves based upon the environment we started in, then we greatly limit our choices and the beauty of the world we have yet to experience.

No matter where in society or in your family tree you are, your value as a human soul is constant. No one is more or less valuable based upon their neighborhood, family's wealth, intelligence, or appearance. As a soul, you are always the ice cream, no matter where you are geographically or socially. And, all ice cream is good.

Although our society is based upon a socio-economic value system, that system doesn't value your soul. Or decide how much you value your life. These choices are yours alone to make. If you wish outside systems or other people to set your value, that is your choice.

Each of us starts somewhere. We each have our own starting point at the beginning of our lives. As we look around, we can see where everyone else is standing. Gradually, we notice the particular features of our environment.

It's possible to look at your life solely in the context of your own starting point, without judging it against anyone else's, as a reflection of your worth as a person. Appreciating your life from your own starting point puts you in control of your decisions and your future.

All of the great inspiring success stories chronicle those who have accepted the reality of the square they started in. Those people took stock of their situation, acknowledged the obstacles and advantages, and considered their own abilities and what they had yet to learn. They then started obtaining the skills and temperament they needed to get where they wanted to go.

Just like a road trip, you start somewhere and then plot your course. It doesn't do any good to fantasize about the easy route you would have had if you had started 100 miles to the west. You've got to deal with the terrain that's in front of you.

Within that terrain, you can choose from many routes to the same destination. If you believe that you are not worthy of the life you envision, then you'll pick the hot, sticky route through the poison ivy and rabid bunnies. If you believe you are worthy, you'll find the easier, sunny path with the perfume of flowers wafting in the breeze. The starting and ending points are the same. How much you enjoy the journey depends upon your value of yourself.

There is something to be said about the route through the poison ivy, though. Many people who find themselves with low self-esteem will take the more challenging route to confirm through life experience that they are strong and beautiful. Sure, they come out with a rash, but they left their low self-esteem back in the bushes. Now, they love themselves enough to make the choice of the easier path that's open to them. Whether they choose it or not is another question. Some people prefer growth through life's extreme challenges. It's the freedom to make the choice that they were after, not necessarily the easier path.

Wherever on your path you find yourself, you can plot a different course to the same destination. One you can enjoy more – whatever enjoyment means to you. You always have a choice. Start seeing yourself as the one with the map, saying, "Taking this route isn't working; what do I need to do to create a better one? I would like to:

1. *Get my degree in engineering.*

2. *Eat foods that make me feel good.*

3. *Find someone I can have fun with.*

4. *Take singing lessons.*

5. *Get out of this relationship.*

"Okay, now I can plan my new route."

I realize that this sounds easier than it is. My goal for you isn't that you change your life or make any new decisions. My goal is only to remind you that *you can*. I'm not interested in your being a better person for some abstract reason. I am interested in your remembering that *you have the choice*. You have free will. You are a soul with authority over the details of your life.

Chapter 3 Exercise

You are HERE.

This exercise gives you some perspective on where you are in relationship to where you've been, where you're headed, and, if you wish to change course, to get where you want to go. Take this as lightly as possible; otherwise, you'll get bogged down in the emotion of your past experiences... which may lead to a nap, a fifth of gin, or a large pizza with extra cheese.

Take as much time as you need. One of my students did it in 30 minutes, while another took four months. Whatever it takes. Being able to objectively and compassionately look at your life will allow you the freedom to make decisions based upon where you wish to go, not based upon the pain from your travels.

Step 1:

Where do I wish to be in my life?

Write out the answer to this question. Put it at the top center of a letter-size paper or larger.

Step 2:

Describing the landscape of your life.

You will need a pencil, a pen, crayons, or paints for this exercise. If you need another creative option, you can cut out pictures from magazines to make a collage, or you can write out a description of your landscape instead.

Focusing on your entire life or just a part of it.

If you would like to focus on one area of your life, such as your career or love life, you can go through the same steps of this exercise.

Read through the four points below before starting this project.

1. *Imagine the life you've lived up to this moment as a landscape with a path meandering through it. What kind of landscape features would your life have: rolling hills, mountains, swamps, streams, forests, oak tree groves, monsters, thieves, hurricanes? How would your path lay out in this landscape? You can be as colorful as you wish to be. And, you can let your life drawing take on a life of its own as you proceed through this exercise.*

2. *Decide where the start of your life (your birth) is in your landscape. From that point, draw your path through the landscape. No matter where the path ends, it's okay. You are getting a sense of where you are.*

3. *Think about the main events of your life. How did each event affect the direction of your path through the landscape?*

4. *Consider the influence of your childhood, parents' love, friends' influence, main events/experiences that shaped your life.*

Step 3:

Once you've drawn the path up to the present, take a look at where you are in your landscape. Notice any patterns of how you learn and create your steps. For instance, you may get experience in three completely different jobs/careers, one right after another. It may not make sense to you or anyone in your life, but you feel compelled to do it. Then, you get a cool job or start a business that incorporates all three types of skills. Or, you may notice patterns with your relationships ("Wow, all my boyfriends have had red hair...") – all seem the same – but as you look, you see an evolution that has made you a stronger person ("...but, they've been nicer guys each time."). Be objective. Pretend you are looking at someone else's landscape. Look at it upside-down, maybe.

Make notes about your observations somewhere on the map or on a separate paper.

Step 4:

Ask yourself these questions:

1. *How close am I to where I wish to be?*

2. *What main events/relationships really changed my course for the better?*

3. *What main events/relationships really changed my course for the worse?*

4. *How would I like to change course, if at all?*

5. *What kinds of decisions do I need to make to get where I wish to be?*

Step 5:

Write out at least three new decisions that support where you wish to go in your life's landscape. Display your map in your home somewhere that you can see it every day.

Step 6:

Make these decisions now and in the days ahead.

No matter what your life is like,

it's **your life**.

You are **choosing** each moment,

regardless of whether you **believe**

you are or not.

You can always **chart** a new course,

or make a new **plan**;

your **life** is yours to **live**.

Four

Yeah, he was my soul mate,
but he never picked up his socks.

Every day we choose the small damaging thing over the big beautiful thing. We dissolve long friendships over gossip. We end marriages over money. We choose pain over love. We give up what we wish for most because it didn't meet our expectations of true love.

When I say we choose the small thing, I mean we choose to hold on to it. You may never speak about it, or let it ruin dinner, but you keep it within your heart, within your relationship. You don't realize the tradeoff. To make room for the pain, you let a little love go.

In that moment of choosing the small thing, you have chosen against your partner. You have chosen to put your partner on the other side of the pain. Now, you and your partner are on opposite sides of pain, instead of side by side in love.

You can always change this, but you must do something different. This requires being honest with yourself and, in some cases, with the person you're in a relationship with. You've got to say to yourself, "I am holding on to all the times my wife belittled me in public." Now what? How important is holding on to this? Would you like to talk with her about it so she can understand how her behavior affects you? Or do you now think it's silly and can just let it go? Does her behavior really bring up something else that's not related to her at all? Is this issue really about your relationship with your mother? Be prepared to discover something new about yourself in this process.

One of my favorite stories is of a husband who would often go to the sink to find a glass or dish his wife hadn't rinsed. No matter how cheerful his mood before, once he saw the dirty dish he would immediately well up with frustration and ask his wife, "Is it too much to ask to rinse your dish!?" In his tone, she could tell that he thought her a complete insensitive slob for leaving the job to him. She would reply, "Well, don't wash it then. There's only three dishes there, just leave them. I'll wash them later. What's the big deal? I could clean the house top to bottom with no comment from you, but if I leave a dish you lose your mind. What's going on?"

What was "going on" was a childhood flashback. The dirty dish stimulated memories of the judgment he felt when his mother would yell at him for not rinsing his dishes. With this new realization, he has the freedom to choose differently. Now, every time he sees his wife's un-rinsed dish, he looks at the dish and says, "Hi Mom, Sarah will wash the dish later." Saying that makes him laugh, reminding himself that he can choose to live in the present moment instead of reliving the pain of 35 years ago. And, it has inspired Sarah to rinse her dishes more often now because she isn't being judged one way or the other.

Love is the natural state of your soul.

Love is the natural state of your soul. You are love – you don't have to hold on to it. Just like you don't have to hold on to your limbs because they are part of you. But, you have to hold on to pain. If you release your grasp, the pain falls – because it's not a natural part of who you are. You're just so accustomed to being in pain that you forget that you are love. You think that love is something you have to find. But, you don't have to search for it… Remove all the Voodoo pins, maybe.

Doing this is simple, but it's not easy. Choosing love over judgment can be one of the most difficult choices we make. It certainly has been one of my life lessons…

My relationship story:
How I almost lost the man of my dreams.

I ended my first marriage of six years when I was 28 years old. Laying out the game plan for my next relationship, I decided that if either one of us couldn't fully accept who the other person really was then we shouldn't be together. I had learned this lesson the hard way in my first marriage. There was nothing wrong with my first husband, but our relationship was based largely upon expectation and judgment. Not enough to build a lasting relationship on.

For my new plan, I reorganized the priorities. I moved "acceptance for who I am" to the top of the list. I was looking for someone who wouldn't judge me. Who would value me as the person I was, not who they hoped I could be. What I didn't consider while I was forming this plan was how I would be challenged in living up to my end of the bargain – could I accept the person who could accept me!

You know the phrase, "She wouldn't know a... if it walked up and bit her"? Well, in 1990, the most amazing, wonderful man did walk up to me and introduce himself. And, he could have bit me, but it wouldn't have made any difference. My judgments about myself, and what I thought I deserved, were so strong that it took me what seemed like forever to realize that he was the person I was looking for. Anyway, here's the story...

While I was separated and waiting for my divorce to settle, I became friends with a man at the company where I had a summer work contract. I liked that he never focused on my physical appearance. I liked that he never bragged about himself, but would tell great stories about his life, giving equal billing to everyone involved. He had a sharp, insightful sense of humor, but wasn't cynical. He took a genuine interest in who I was and what I had to say. I could tell he was a giving person.

Of course, I couldn't consider him for a serious relationship. He wore big accountant tortoise-shell glasses, high-water polyester pants, a homemade haircut from his best friend's mom, and dorky sport coats. I'm sorry, but the only guys I fall for are big, charismatic chick magnets – and this guy wasn't it... not by a thousand miles.

It took me three months to realize that this work friend was the love of my life. Sure, I was a little dense, but I didn't expect him to be wearing a disguise. Only after I realized that he had accepted me the first day we met, was I able to see him without the filters of my judgments.

I'm telling you this story because that moment was humbling and self-revealing in many ways. I realized a few things.

First, because of the limits I placed on myself and what I could experience, I almost lost him. My disapproval was obvious to him, and he was about to give up on me. How many of my dreams had I already shunned because they didn't arrive in the expected package? I didn't even want to know.

Second, acceptance would always be a choice I had to think twice about since self-ridicule and ridicule of others so shaped my childhood years. I would and still do constantly check myself for my automatic response to judge a person or experience.

Third, I realized that I could have all the passionate heat, charisma, and drama I wanted, but without acceptance, there is no love… of myself, or of the other person. Without acceptance, judgment would eventually end all of my relationships prematurely.

My work friend turned into my life-partner and husband for the last 18 years. We have a total blast generally, but we have had a few intense arguments along the way. Each one was a learning experience about choosing the small thing or the big beautiful thing.

The small thing vs. the big beautiful thing.

I remember one such argument in the kitchen. He was standing in front of the refrigerator with the door magnet poem I had assembled for him the day before – "Sticky honey monkey toes" – visible over his left shoulder. I was facing him at the end of the counter in my lavender fleece bathrobe. I don't recall the argument, but I do remember saying to myself, "Wow, I'm against my husband right now, and how I'm discussing this problem is driving us apart. He's worth more to me than winning the fight. We can only solve the problem together anyway, not apart." I dropped my defenses. I stopped reflexively trying to win and be right. I asked him if we could start over – that as much as I hoped to win this argument, I loved him more and would rather understand his point of view than just shove mine down his throat.

In other arguments since, I've had to ask myself, "What am I not accepting within myself or within him that is creating this lack of communication?" We're always going to have problems, but if I'm not his partner at his side solving them together, then where am I? And, how do I get back?

One of our ongoing favorite arguments is about money. He's a very good, conservative money manager, and I'm a high-risk entrepreneur. Currently, we make an excellent team. We just had to work out a few, uh… kinks along the way. On the surface the issue was financial. But, the arguments weren't really about money, but about fears and insecurities about ourselves. That being the case, each of us entered the argument fighting an internal battle – just two dogs howling at the moon. We never resolved anything.

Gradually, we understood what was happening – we didn't know ourselves or each other as well as we thought we did. Instead of holding on to our fears that would eventually drive us apart, we decided to listen and learn.

We started by setting time aside in our week for "listen and learn" counseling sessions with each other. One session I would talk and he would listen and learn. The next session, we reversed roles. Each of us had our turn. After a couple of years, we integrated these talks into our daily routine, discussing our deepest fears about money, sex, and life paths while we ate breakfast or folded clothes from the wash.

These counselings gave each of us the safety and freedom to uncover our fears and judgments without the expectation of having a real-world problem to solve. Quickly, they became important building blocks for our relationship. When problems did arise, we approached them together as challenges to address, not a battle of blame we'd fight against each other.

In your important relationships, how much do you accept yourself and the other person? How many times have you chosen the small thing over the big beautiful thing? This next exercise is designed to help you acknowledge how you've built the foundation of your relationship, and how you can use that strong foundation to work with each other side by side in love.

Chapter 4 Exercise

Side by side in love.

For this exercise you'll need two letter-size pieces of paper or larger, a pencil, and an eraser.

Step 1:

Choose which relationship you'd like to work with. At the top of the page, write down the person's name and the type of relationship you have with them (e.g., husband, wife, brother, boss, sister, etc.).

Step 2:

Divide the paper into three columns:

| *"Love It"* | *"Drives Me Nuts"* | *"Why"* |

In the "Love It" column, write down the best parts of your relationship. In the "Drives Me Nuts" column, write down the worst parts of your relationship.

Step 3:

In the "Why" column, write down why you feel the way you do. Here's an example:

Love It:

He's always excited about hugging me.

Drives Me Nuts:

> *Sometimes he turns off the light when he leaves a room even if I'm still in it.*

Why:

> *Love It: Every time I can tell he loves me, and that he loves himself and our relationship.*

> *Drives Me Nuts: My first reaction is that he doesn't know I exist. But, I really know it's because he does many things on automatic.*

Step 4:

On the second sheet of paper titled with the person's name and the relationship type, make three columns:

To lighten the mood, you can draw a little cartoon character of how you look when you are stuck on the small thing, and what you look like when you are enjoying the big beautiful thing.

"Small Thing"   "Big Beautiful Thing"   "New Decision/Behavior"

In the "Small Thing" column, write out your fear/judgment/expectation/sadness that surfaces when the other person does the thing that drives you nuts.

In the "Big Beautiful Thing" column, write out what part of your love or acceptance of yourself or the other person the small thing is blocking.

In the third column, write out the new choice you are going to make so you can be side by side addressing this problem, instead of putting this problem between you. It's possible that your new decision will be a change in behavior on your part that doesn't require any discussion. Other types of problems will require the two of you working in supportive partnership to solve it. When you introduce the subject, talk about how the other person's behavior affects you rather than point out that their behavior is wrong. You will be much more successful. Remember, the goal is to do this side by side. No one is going to be right in this discussion, but you both can be loved.

Here's an example:

Small Thing:

> I think he doesn't know I exist.

Big Beautiful Thing:

> That he does love me. My existence doesn't depend upon how other people treat me. There's nothing malicious in his behavior. He's just on autopilot and on to the next thing in his mind.

New Decision/Behavior:

> Laugh about it. Don't make him feel bad. Make it easier for him to forgive himself and for me to realize that there's really no problem.

Change and success.

Over the days and weeks, notice how your behavior and the behavior of others have changed. Refer back to your notes of this exercise. You may be surprised by how different things are now. Celebrate the smallest shift, because no shift is small.

*You choose who **you are**.*

No past experience

*has the **power** to shape you*

*unless you **choose it** so.*

*You can **let go**.*

Five

Finding grace in your missteps.

We tend to downplay our mistakes and highlight our successes. In our downplaying, we may sweep under the rug the consequences of our missteps. Try to forget our actions so we can just move on. When we do this, we devalue our life and the lives of those affected by our decisions.

Treating each misstep as important an action as a correct step acknowledges the value of all your thoughts and movements. Doing so gives you an opportunity to reflect, understand, and repair relationships. Admitting and valuing a mistake can deepen trust within you and with others. Grace is possible in those moments of honoring your actions and their effects.

Our society holds very strong beliefs around mistakes and penance for those mistakes. Most of the time, when we publicly acknowledge our missteps, and value the growth we gained through the experience, we are forgiven. The burden is lifted and our lives are richer. These guidelines for understanding the gravity of doing harm to others intentionally or unintentionally play a valuable role in our lives. It is when we are not forgiven, when our mistakes are used to manipulate us, that we have a new set of choices to make.

Each of us has the capacity to forgive. Love and forgiveness go hand-in-hand. Forgiveness brushes away obstacles between people. Blame comes between them. When a person chooses not to forgive, they are telling you they are choosing the pain of your mistake over their love for you. From that point forward, the pain they choose to keep will color their communication with you. Whether or not you forgive them is your choice. Whether or not to forgive yourself is your choice, too.

Story of two brothers.

I know of two adult brothers who had difficult childhoods. When they were still kids, their parents' divorce split up the family, forcing them to take sides and live in separate homes. Each did and said hurtful things to the other through the years in an effort to cope with the aftermath of their family falling apart. At times, forgiveness was impossible on both sides. They fell into a cycle of blame and regret with each other. The sadness from losing their childhood relationship seemed irreconcilable.

Slowly, through their 20s and 30s, they talked it all out, putting their childhood motivations in perspective. Together they learned how to restore their relationship, separating it from the emotional roller coaster of their youth. They stopped blaming each other so they could have the relationship they loved as kids. Each had to forgive themselves and each other for all things, not just some of them. In this process, they found compassion for their past actions and came to a much deeper understanding of each other's life.

Understanding why you made the choices you did, then growing from that knowledge, is different from living with your mistakes. As the two brothers discovered, living with your mistakes doesn't get you where you wish to go – you just end up living with them as if they were bad roommates you can't evict.

The only thing you can count on is that if you do hold on to your mistakes or someone else's, you're more likely to repeat the behavior. Which, interestingly, fulfills the prophecy that you are doomed by your mistakes and doomed to have people make the same mistakes with you that you can't forgive. You're only doomed if you keep them… It's kind of like how your love life would be doomed if all of your ex-lovers tagged along on your dates!

Your decisions shape your life, but they don't shape you.

Anyone who tells you differently is trying to exert control over you. You are not a screw-up, or bad at relationships, or untrustworthy. You are *you* – an eternal soul with the ability to learn and the power to choose. Your actions do have value and should be acknowledged for the effect they have on yourself and others. These actions are your tools for understanding yourself, not weapons to be used against you.

You have chosen to explore your life through trial and error, learning as you go, but you are not these experiences. You are an eternal soul making choices as a method of understanding how to express yourself clearly. Honoring all of your actions comes from the grace of your soul.

Chapter 5 Exercise

Understanding your misstep, then lifting the burden.

I recommend you do this exercise as if you were cleaning someone else's house. Identifying the useless knick-knacks and old mementos that make the house look cluttered and unappealing is easy to do in someone else's house, right? So, assume the role of a friend whose been asked to help throw stuff out.

Use a letter-size paper or larger, a pen or pencil, and crayons or colored pencils, if you like.

Step 1:

Divide the paper into three columns:

"Mistake/Year"   *"Holding On"*   *"Replace With"*

Step 2:

In the "Mistake/Year" column, write down the mistake that still burdens you, and the year you made it.

Step 3:

In the "Holding On" column, write out how the consequences of this decision affect your ability to make better decisions in your life now. Ask yourself, "Is there anything more I can do about this?" If the answer is "no," then let it go. If the answer is "yes," define what you are going to do and your plan for doing it. Then, let the burden go as a way of closing the book on that life experience. Then, move forward with your plan.

Step 4:

In the "Replace With" column, write out what emotion, behavior, or belief you'd like to have in your life instead.

Step 5:

Now, tear or cut the paper into two pieces. One piece has the first two columns, and the second piece has the last, "Replace With" column.

Step 6:

Happily, and with gusto, rip up the piece of paper with the "Mistake/Year" and "Holding On" columns.

Step 7:

Somewhere in your home, tape up the remaining "Replace With" column so you can remember your new choices.

Step 8:

Do one thing every day that supports your new choices. Notice what changes occur in your life because you let go of old mistakes and have embraced new adventures.

It takes **strength** to live your life.

You came into this **life** with

the strength you **need**.

Call on it,

and it will **come**.

Six | Choices –
new and improved!

Yyou can regain control of your ability to make better choices even if you've made poor choices that you feel compelled to repeat and believe you can't change. Doing so will require you to take an inventory of the choices you have allowed yourself to make. Then, decide what kinds of decisions you'd like to replace them with.

I'm aware that we're talking about decisions made in highly emotional situations. I realize we make decisions based upon past intensely emotionally charged life experiences; however, if we're serious about giving ourselves more alternatives to choose from, we have to step back and find a way to look at our situation with more objectivity.

Imagine that you are a shopkeeper. On your store shelves sit – like dusty boxes and soda cans – the choices you've made, plus the choices sold to you by other people, and the choices that came with the store. Some choices are popular. A few are cheap and poorly made. Several reflect your tastes. Others don't, but they're family favorites. If you are a shopkeeper who rushes in a minute or two before the doors open and then rushes out at closing time, you probably have just enough time to re-order the same old stuff people are buying regardless of profit margin. You will keep your head above water financially, but there won't be much growth or adventure.

If, on the other hand, you are a shopkeeper who gets in early, rotates the merchandise, researches better products, plans the store's future, purges old inventory, develops products that really express who you are, and finds customers who would love your custom products, then your store will grow and be identified with you as unique and valuable.

The choices of your life are as tangible as the merchandise on a store's shelves. You can discard items, invent others, set prices, tailor products to each customer, take your time deciding which one is right for each customer, and so on. You can continually re-evaluate and make changes to them. What causes us to consider our choices permanent fixtures instead of items we can remove and replace are the emotional memories that surround them.

Here's an example of a store inventory that needs to be rotated:

A customer comes into your store and asks, "Excuse me, sir, what is that on the top shelf?" You reply, "Oh, I first stocked that item when I was eight. It reminds me that I agreed with my brother that I'm not very smart so he won't feel threatened and ridicule me in public. My brother is the only one who buys it."

We make these types of choices for the sake of love for another, usually under duress or caught off guard in a situation with no time to think through the other's motivations. Sometimes, someone else brings the choice into the store, as in this case with your brother. He muscled it in and said, "This is what I want. You're going to sell it to me cheap every time I come in." Now, each time you sell him this product, it increases the difficulty of presenting him with something different.

There is another choice. (There's always another choice!) To find that choice, you'll have to come into the store early, do some research, probably invent a custom choice that allows you to both be true to yourself and handle your brother's insecurity issues. You might replace it with a pride-filled acknowledgement about his life's accomplishments or strengths without belittling your own. Next time he comes in demanding his product, you offer him a new one: "Hi, do you have time for lunch this week? I'd like to learn more about the Fun Run you're organizing this summer."

When you start offering new choices to your customers – the people in your life – you may find that you lose some of them as well as gain new ones. That's part of the process. It's *your* store. It's your life. You'll have to decide if you are worth going to this kind of trouble. By doing so, you are choosing to recognize your value as a human soul.

You have the strength to remove your burdens.

Removing from the shelf a past choice covered in emotion will require your steady, loving hand. Just know that your same hand that accepted the choice has the strength to remove it. This strength is that of your soul.

Just as you use the strength of your body to place or remove an item from a shelf, you use the strength of your soul to place or remove a burden within you. Both are actions of your soul. No one can give you a burden without your accepting it. Your belief that you have no choice but to accept it is the same belief that says you do not have the choice to remove it. Both can be false, if you wish.

This can be a sticking point for many people. Believe me when I tell you that making a choice that carries a burden with it requires the strength of your soul. And the strength you used to accept the pain is the only strength you need to release it. When you reach for the choice and you feel the weight within you, acknowledge that you needed strength to put it there. To make a different choice, call upon that strength. It will come.

Chapter 6 Exercise

Swapping out old merchandise.

This exercise is very thorough and will take some time. Make sure you have water and a snack. This exercise will address one choice (product). You can repeat the exercise for every choice you'd like to change.

You may find that you can't think of any choices right now – your mind's blank. So, just allow yourself to be aware over the next hours/days when you do something you don't wish to do, whether out of obligation, extortion, fear, and so on. Then, make a mental note or write it down so you can refer to it later when you start this exercise.

The reason we find it difficult to make simple changes in our lives is that the change isn't about what we think it's about. The change is never about eating right, going to bed early, asking for the raise at work. With each change you make, you are choosing expression over suppression. You, in that small change, are freeing your soul. Always respect the strength it takes to make the smallest change – because no change is small. That's what makes change so rewarding. You see the change in every part of your life, not just the part you are focused on!

Following is a completed sample exercise for you to read through to get a sense of how to do it.

Step 1:

Identifying current choice and preferred choice.

> **Current Choice:** *I stay up late on weeknights.*
>
> **Consequence:** *I wake up tired and late, then I rush around. I'm scattered all day at work.*
>
> **Preferred Choice:** *Make my lunch the night before, go to bed early.*
>
> **Consequence:** *Wake up on time and rested. Have time to eat breakfast. Have a better, calmer day.*

Step 2:

Current Choice emotional weight

Current Choice questions:

> 1. **What goes through your head when you battle between the choices?** *The next day will suck, so I might as well stay up and enjoy tonight as long as I can.*
>
> 2. **What emotions do you feel?** *Sadness, rebellion.*
>
> 3. **What is the rationalization you come up with to decide the current choice is better than the desired choice?** *That I'm having fun and I can always wake up early to get to work on time.*

Current Choice Consequences questions:

> 1. **What do you tell yourself you'll do to make the current choice work?** *I can get up early enough this time. I want to relax more, not just go to sleep.*

2. ***How do you feel after you experience the consequences of the current decision?*** *I realize the day is going to suck because I'm tired and late for work.*

3. ***What kind of self-image does this decision reinforce?*** *I'm not very good at living my life, and happiness probably won't happen for me.*

4. ***Who is happy that you are failing at enjoying this part of your life?*** *My parents.*

5. ***Can you remember when you decided to accept this burden of making this person feel better by you not loving yourself?*** *When I was a kid. When I would have too much fun, my parents would tell me to enjoy it while I could because when I grew up the fun would be over.*

Step 3:

Preferred Choice emotional weight

Preferred Choice questions:

1. ***What do you fear will occur if you make the preferred choice?*** *I'll realize I actually like my job and that being happy is much easier than my family said it would be. I'll feel like I've disobeyed my family's beliefs.*

2. ***What belief do you have to let go of in order to make this choice?*** *That I can't be happier than my parents. And that only through hard work can life be rewarding.*

Preferred Choice Consequences questions:

1. **What kind of self-image does this preferred decision reinforce?** *That I care about myself and that I'm worth caring for.*

2. **Who is happy that you are succeeding at enjoying this part of your life?** *My roommate and I.*

3. **What burden is lifted?** *The belief that happiness isn't possible.*

4. **What is your true belief about happiness and success?** *Happiness is taking care of myself and doing things that make my life easier and stronger.*

Step 4:

Adding your new product to the shelf.

Next time you are ready to make this choice, give yourself time to read through your answers so you can remember why the new one is going to work much better for you.

Be on the lookout for a new self-image.

Knowing you have strength and willpower for the changes you wish to make does wonders for your self-esteem. You may find yourself walking around as if you have superpowers (which you do!). You may need to find a cape and tights in your size, just in case.

You are not flawed.

You are not a **diamond**

made **worthless** by cracks

running through it.

You are the sun **shining** through

the **weather** of your life.

The **day** may be cold or dark,

but you are always the **sun**.

Seven

Why some habits are easier to break than others.

I n the previous chapter I suggested that you could give yourself the option of making a new choice. I also offered an exercise for discovering the emotions or beliefs tied to the decisions we wish to change. Now I will go into a little more detail about why some behaviors and habits are so much easier to change than others.

Let's say you have two power lines. One is a low 12-volt cell phone charger plugged into your home wall socket. The other is a 100-megawatt transformer that feeds electricity to the city grid. Which line can you cut while power is still running through it – and survive?

Your ability to survive cutting the transformer line has nothing to do with your character or your strength. It has everything to do with the amount of juice running through the line. As long as you turn off the power to the transformer, you'll be fine. The method for changing a behavior is similar. Understanding how much power is flowing into the habit, then finding the source so you can turn it off, is the key. Otherwise, you're toast – burnt toast.

Breaking a habit requires free will, not willpower.

How much have you beaten yourself up for not being able to make what you think is a simple change? Very few self-destructive habits require simple changes. And, rarely is breaking the habit a matter of willpower.

Successfully breaking a habit requires that you understand why you established the habit in the first place. More than likely you adopted this behavior as an emotional protection or painkiller, or to bury deep-seated fears. There are other reasons, too, but these are a few of the main ones.

In order to change your behavior, you've got to change your mind about how to respond to whatever was happening at the time of the original decision. Which means you will need to remember what the original situation was, so you can change that decision. That's why breaking a habit isn't about willpower. Because the will you are going up against is your own – your will "now" versus your will "at the time" you chose to form the habit as a way of coping with the situation.

Following the habit to its source.

Let's say, for example, that you have a weight problem, but you only overeat at home. At work and elsewhere you are fine. In your own kitchen you mow through your groceries like a locust. You do not have a willpower problem. What you have is a decision you made when you were five years old on how to emotionally handle your parents fighting all the time. You couldn't leave. You couldn't say anything. You couldn't cry or make a fuss. In trying to find a way to feel good, and calm your body down, you figured out that food did the trick. You were too young to solve it any other way. Now you're 35 years old, operating off a 5-year-old's decision about emotional coping. And, that 5-year-old has much at stake in her behavior. She's going to power that behavior with everything she's got, which doesn't leave much left over for new, better behavior.

Turning off the power to the habit.

Instead of fighting the 100-megawatt willpower of a scared 5-year-old, you can gently reassure this child that your present-day home is safe. In this conversation, or set of conversations, many other emotions and issues will surface, which is a good thing. You are freeing yourself of a decision that no longer serves you, but likely saved your sanity back then. You are also redirecting your willpower from the childhood decision to a new one you wish to make now.

Judging your integrity or value as a person because you overeat doesn't make sense anymore when you discover why you do it. Now you have the opportunity of freeing yourself from the echo of your past while celebrating the safe, harmonious home you created for yourself. (However, if you live in a home with a similar level of strife as your childhood home, then you have just discovered a big piece of the puzzle on how you can be happy.)

Until you acknowledge and value the decisions you've already made, you won't be able to stop your will from fueling that decision. And, you won't be able to make new ones. It is the strength of your love for yourself that won't let you devalue a past choice. You will stay right where you are until you recognize that you did the best you could at the time. That scared kid will not stop eating the brownies until someone comes and tells her everything is okay now, and that she did a good job. Your problem isn't that you don't have power – you've got plenty. Remembering what decisions you've made in the past that are still drawing power from your own will is key to freeing your will to choose new behaviors.

How many times have you heard friends and family say that the habit they face is too much for them, or that the temptation was too great? Remember that the formidable power they face is their own. They are staring at the power of a choice they made. Until they allow themselves to acknowledge the value of the original choice they made, breaking the habit will be nearly impossible.

Changing your choices to fit your current understanding of yourself.

Think of it as upgrading a software program. When something in your life is not working, look for the choice that is now out of date, understand why you made it, let it go (which may take some time), then, carefully and full of acceptance, allow yourself to get used to the new decisions you wish to make for that part of your life. You are growing and evolving all the time. It stands to reason that you'll need to upgrade your behavior as you find better ways to live your life. Maybe now's the time to check.

Chapter 7 Exercise

Accepting what you consider a bad habit now as the best idea you had back then.

For this exercise, you'll need a few sheets of letter-size paper or larger, a pencil or pen, and crayons or colored pencils.

Step 1:

On one sheet, write out the answers to the following questions:

1. *What habit/behavior do you wish to change?*

2. *Why do you wish to change it? How does it affect your life?*

3. *What behavior/habit would you like to put in its place?*

4. *At what age or how many years ago did you start the habit/ behavior?*

5. *What was happening in your life at the time? Do you remember the situation that triggered it?*

6. *If you do remember, then write down what you felt your choices were at the time.*

7. *At the time, how did adopting this behavior help you cope with the situation?*

8. *Does this situation still exist in your life? If not, how did you resolve it?*

9. *Or, are you in a similar situation now that reinforces the habit?*

    a. *If you are, then what first step can you take to change your environment to one that supports the habit you would like to put in its place?*

    b. *If you are not, then how does your current situation support the habit/behavior you'd like to put in its place?*

Step 2:

For this next part, think of yourself as behaving as two different people. The "Now" version, who has a better way of coping with the issue, and the "Then" version, who is still coping at the age you were when it all started.

(In the exercise below, draw yourself as stick figures. Don't worry about artistic ability. These are representational, not realistic.)

On another sheet of paper, you are going to draw a picture of the "Then" you. Are you a scared little girl huddled under the kitchen table... or maybe a defiant teenager protecting his honor... or a young soldier in battle...?

Step 3:

On this page somewhere, write out some emotional characteristics of this person. Look at this person you've drawn as they face the original situation. At the time, what other choices did you consider? Remember why you rejected those other choices and felt this one was the safest to make.

Step 4:

On another sheet of paper, draw a picture of the "Now" you.

Step 5:

On this page somewhere, write out some emotional characteristics of the person you are now. Look at this person you've drawn. What choices do you have now that you didn't have back then to deal with the same situation? Write out the choice you would make now.

Step 6:

On this page with the "Now" you, draw the "Then" you next to it. This time, before you draw, tell the "Then" you that the "Now" you will make all the decisions and they can just relax. Okay, now draw.

You can see that what you are doing is helping a fearful part of you realize that the threat no longer exists, and that a smart, caring adult (you) is in charge. As the days pass, you may find that you'll need to reassure yourself that there is no need for the behavior because the danger is gone. Slowly, the emotional trigger will subside. If it doesn't, then you may wish the further support of a counselor or a trusted friend.

We may have,

*in our everyday **challenges**,*

*convinced **ourselves** that the*

***beautiful** choice is not possible.*

But, it is there,

*resting **lightly** beside our judgments,*

*humming **quietly** amongst our fears,*

*floating **peacefully** around us,*

*waiting for us to **choose it**.*

Eight

You dream your own dream.

No matter what kind of life you lead, it has value beyond any social or cultural standards. You may have devalued the life you're living in favor of what society values as worthy or successful. This social pressure can persuade you to give up the life you wish to live as a soul. When you do this, your life becomes difficult, unfulfilling, and empty. The "good life" may be good, but it's not the right life for you.

There is a woman working as a cashier at a Kansas discount superstore. As a soul, she wished a simple, anonymous life to explore her inner self in a way she couldn't if her life was more stressful or complicated. Should we assess this woman's value and her ability to create a successful life according to the social standard? She's a cashier. She's a little overweight. She's not a beauty queen. She's a bit of a wallflower. Do we rate her life a 3 on a scale of 1 to 10? How does she rate her own life? Does she have enough of a sense of herself to appreciate the life she created?

You chose to experience yourself in a very specific way in your physical life. Fitting into an acceptable or stereotypical successful lifestyle will not work for you. Period.

When you abandon your soul's desire in favor of conforming to social standards, you can quickly lose your sense of yourself. Without realizing it, you have chosen to judge your dream as inappropriate. When you encounter a person different from you, this judgment surfaces. Your judgment of someone else is a reflection of a judgment you have of yourself – where you have accepted the social standard or someone else's standard instead of your own life's vision.

Around you are people who can think and act in ways you believe you cannot. When you remember we are all souls with the capacity for expression of all things, then you can consider letting go of the fears and judgments that constrict your expression. Now the opportunity to find your freedom and your dream stands before you. The person you find yourself judging can help you understand a part of your life. If possible, engage them in conversation. Learn about who they are and what they believe. Every single time, you will find new acceptance of yourself – a new part of your life that you can appreciate.

Nothing is more important than your vision of your life. Your appearance, education, personality, and intelligence do not increase or decrease the value of your life or your passion to live it. And, no one else in the world today sees life the way you do. Right now, someone is trying to put the pieces of their life together and your point of view is the key. They don't know it, but you're what they need. We have each other's answers because we're all living different parts of the total human experience.

Chapter 8 Exercise

Judgment challenge: Extreme compassion required!

Step 1:

For this exercise, observe what you ridicule or whom you pass judgment on during the day. Make a note of it.

Step 2:

At the end of the day, review your notes. Do they have a theme? How do these judgments apply to you? Maybe you judge people who laugh all the time as being irresponsible. Does this reflect how your happiness was suppressed in your life?

Note that this exercise isn't designed for you to agree with the other person's behavior or beliefs. This is designed for you to find where you are not free to express yourself. The judgment of another isn't really about the conflicting beliefs or behaviors between the two of you; it's about conflicting beliefs within yourself.

So, be as gentle as possible. The harsher you judge another's action, the stronger the judgment is within yourself. And, this method of reflection may lead to surprising places.

Step 3:

Talking out your findings with a friend or recording them.

You may find talking over your notes and observations with a friend to be helpful. Most likely, you've had this judgment about yourself for a long time. And, you know you've already rationalized it under your mental rug to avoid the real issue. By using the tool of talking out loud, you can hear your thoughts on the open air instead of swimming around in your head. You'll be amazed at how objective you can be when you voice your thoughts to yourself.

Step 4:

Now the tricky part: doing what you love.

1.   *What judgment did you discover that you accepted about yourself?*

2.   *What part of you has been unexpressed all this time?*

3.   *How can you integrate this part of you in your life?*

Step 5:

Enjoying your new expression.

For this step, especially, you've got to find a way to laugh at yourself. You've taken a sow's ear and turned it into a silk purse. Consider your other judgments a goldmine of your beautiful self hidden within!

Next time you realize you are judgmental, yell, "JACKPOT!"

Every soul is a **truth**.

Each soul is a different truth.

All souls are part of

the **same truth**.

Nine

The moment we all live for.

A moment we've all had. A moment at once freeing, joyful, and painful. A moment great novels and movies revolve around. *The turning point in a person's life.* In your life. The moment someone pauses in the forward motion of a typical day, looks directly at you, into you, then acknowledges that you are not just a body handing them coffee or a piece of paper.

They see past your physical appearance, insecurities, quality of your clothes, and past your mistakes, failures, cruelties, fears, social status – they skip it all – straight to the beautiful part of you shining through the weather of your life.

The moment someone recognizes you to the depth of your soul. The moment when time stops, your heart expands, old pain stirs then melts away. You remember who you are. That you are not just a body going through the motions of your day. You are more.

These moments that we give each other are wonderful. You may not know why, but you feel great. You forget your problems for a second, just seeing all the possibilities within you.

All of us secretly wish for the day when we're brave enough to let ourselves have that moment.

Chapter 9 Exercise

Creating the moment.

Sometime during your day, stop for a moment. Take a slow breath. Feel your feet on the ground. Feel the sun on your head. Feel the air on your face. Look around you. Watch people live their lives for a few minutes. Remember, they are doing what you are doing. They're trying to love themselves, and trying to love through what they do with their lives.

Catch someone's eye. Smile with this compassion and understanding.

As you go through your day, take time to acknowledge the value in the small interactions you have with people.

We all want what you want. We all have what each other needs. Let it shine through.

I am here, **growing** your vegetables.

I am here, **writing** you a ticket.

I am here, totally **ignoring** you.

I am here, **marrying** you.

I am here, **singing** you a song.

I am here, **giving** you my order.

I am here, **hoping** you see me.

Ten

Life Mechanics
for everyday living.

When I was a kid, I took apart our toaster, my ten-speed bike, my walkie-talkie, and to my parents' dismay, the telephone. I dissected plants and dead bugs. I liked understanding how things worked. Over time, one playful, persistent observation held true: Everything is everything.

Meaning that virtually everything man-made is based upon the structure or function of the human body. And the human body is based upon the structure of an energy body. Just like the physical body is made up of molecules and the molecules are composed of atoms and so on, there is a body for the soul. The body for the soul is constructed of light and form and holds our thoughts, dreams, and memories.

Early on in my life, I became interested in the mechanics of our lives, thoughts, habits, and personalities. If I could take apart a toaster, I could take apart my fear of not being perfect, to understand why that thought existed and how it worked. Later on in my training, I confirmed that you could hold a fear in your hand, balance it on your nose, and then drop it out of your life. In fact, you did this in the very first chapter exercise. Simply and immediately, you let go of thoughts as easily as taking gravel out of ice cream.

Every thought has form. This form is tangible to us. For example, we experience the weight of thoughts as "heavy on the heart," "pressing on my mind," or as "lightening the mood." As souls, we operate within a subtle but cohesive universe of consciousness. We bring our consciousness into our lives at birth. We shape our consciousness with the thoughts we create or accept into our inner life. Our inner life, also called a noetic field, then shapes our lives because we live our lives based upon thoughts.

Although conventional science still holds the position that if consciousness exists it would only be as a byproduct of brain activity, there is leading-edge physics theory that offers an outside-the-brain point of view about the mechanics of consciousness. Physicist Richard Amoroso's work in this area, along with emotional psychology research being done at the Institute of HeartMath, neurologist Mario Beauregard's spiritual brain theory at the University of Montreal, and advancements made by many others, will go far to close the gap between ancient teachings, modern human experience, and existing scientific theory.

A story of Life Mechanics in action.

I'd like to share a story with you that illustrates how simple restoring the fabric of your life can be once you know what to do. While I was at a community center, preparing for a public lecture, a young policewoman walked in and sat down. Clearly, she wasn't there in a professional capacity or she wouldn't have just found a chair and settled in. I walked over, introduced myself, and we started chatting. She explained that she was called out to the center on a tripped alarm somewhere. Nothing came of it, so she had a few minutes before dispatch sent her on another call. She felt drawn to come in, so she did.

I asked her to tell me what was going on with her. Relieved, she told me about her marriage coming to an end a few months back, the emotional pain she felt at the time, and her wish that she somehow could avoid the grief of a lost relationship. In that wish, she found herself fast and deeply in love with another man. Always a strong, independent person, she let her defenses down completely and allowed him to enter the center of her heart in hopes that he'd erase her grief. But the relationship ended quickly and badly, with him treating her rather cruelly on an emotional level. Two months had passed since their breakup and she hadn't been the same. She went on to explain that she'd lost the confidence she'd enjoyed her entire life. She couldn't get him out of her mind and wished on him the same pain he had inflicted on her. Then, she said, "If I could just reach into my heart and get him out, I know I'd feel better." Happily, I replied, "Okay, I'll show you how. Are you ready right now?"

Replying, "Yes," she relaxed a bit. "First," I continued, "you realize that you made the decision to let him in to a place you knew he didn't belong?" She interjected immediately, "Uh, yeah, I know. I just didn't want to admit it. But I knew I shouldn't have let him in that far." "And," I continued, "this place within the heart of your soul is meant only for you. It is the sanctuary where you have your relationship with yourself and with what you consider God. Letting anyone else in there is like inviting a bull into a china shop."

This woman understood. In fact, she had sensed it all along, surmising, "So, he's not really the bad guy, then? And, I'm not the victim. I made a decision at a moment of weakness that started this whole thing. Okay, I get it. I'm ready to forgive him, and not be so hard on myself."

"Alright, then. Rub your hands together. With one hand, reach into your heart and gently gather up the part of his soul that's stuck in there." I watched as she carefully wiggled her fingers in front of her chest; the energy of the man's soul slowly flowing into her hand. Now, with a glowing ball of light in her hands, I asked her to allow it to go back to him by letting the ball float off her hands. She did, and in an instant the ball was gone. Breathing a sigh of relief, she said, "Well, I figure I've got to do that about 30 more times to get it all out."

I replied, "That's what it looks like to me, too. Now, the next step is retrieving the part of your soul you had to move out of the way to make room for him to come in. Cup your hands as if you were getting ready to hold a basketball. Watch as your own energy flows into your hands to form a ball shape. When you think you've got enough, move the gold energy into your heart to fill the space you've opened by removing your ex-lover from the body of your soul."

Smiling, she sighed and said, "Thank you. I knew I could just reach in there, but wasn't sure how. I'll keep doing this until I know it's done." Then, at that moment, her radio went off with a call from dispatch. We hugged, and she left.

This ability of choice allows you to see thoughts, move emotions, store memories, and create visions of your life. Just like the physical body can move products on the store shelves and see the sun on the horizon, so can the soul re-arrange its reality and see into the distance. Throughout this book, you have been reaching into the body of your soul to free yourself of old decisions in order to make new choices. This is a great beginning. You have a better understanding of how the body of the soul is built and how it operates. An understanding you can use every day to live life according to your design.

Much has changed in my life since I began my training in the mechanics of the soul. Prior to that, I felt I had very little control over what happened to me. I would make a plan for the day that by the time I walked out the door in the morning was already changed beyond recognition: a phone call from a friend needing help, forgetting to prepare for a meeting, skipping breakfast, no time to make my lunch. Angry, frustrated, hungry, and late and I hadn't even stepped outside yet. Even though I was an optimistic person, I dreaded every day because I had no way to direct it. I was at the mercy of the unknown forces of my own life.

Now that I understand the mechanics of my life, I can choose how I react to what happens during my day. I can choose how I feel about myself. I can decide how I wish to have relationships with people. I have traveled my own landscape and found the decisions I made in the past, and then changed them to better serve me. More of my time is spent expressing who I am now instead of expressing what I have done before.

You are living a specific life.

Your life has a specific landscape – a unique way of operating. While your challenges and joys find common ground with many other people, your journey and your goals are unique and valuable.

This perspective gives you the freedom to choose differently anytime. To explore, make mistakes, then learn from them without branding yourself with judgment. Remember, you're getting the recipe right – giving yourself time and forgiveness to taste your baking, then make some adjustments and try again.

The best way to approach this new process is playfully. Everything you're going to encounter, as you consider which fear or limitation to address first, will likely be somber and heavy. Everything about you as a soul is lightness and infinite strength. This strength is most effectively expressed through lightness and play. When you combine constructive playfulness and free will, you get fundamental change within your life.

Following is the final exercise in this book. I invite you to use this exercise to acknowledge how much about your life you really do love. What you don't love or what doesn't work requires your loving touch and understanding, both of yourself and those around you. As a soul, your strength is in your gentleness. In your ability to illuminate the truth about your life and your actions resides your power to live your life as you wish.

Chapter 10 Exercise

You can approach this exercise in any way you wish: a written list, collage, song, drawings and murals, sculpture, a one-act play... This is a celebration of your life and how you wish to live it. Do it justice!

1. Ten things I love about my life

2. Ten things I will do to honor and enjoy my life

3. Ten things I wish to understand about my life

4. Ten steps I will take to understand my life

1. Ten things I love about my life.

Write out ten things you love about your life. If you can come up with more, write down as many as you can. If you can only think of one, write it down. As the days pass, you will think of more things you love about your life. When you do, write them down.

2. Ten things I will do to honor and enjoy my life.

Write down at least ten activities you can do within the next week or two that honor and celebrate your life. If you don't feel you have a life worth celebrating, then consider that you are celebrating the life you are about to create. Your first step in creating a life you like is doing things you enjoy that honor your life.

3. Ten things I wish to understand about my life.

What aspects of your life are mysteries to you? Write down as many as you can. You might come up with more as the days pass. That's fine. Write them down as you go along.

4. Ten steps I will take to understand my life.

This may take more time, or it might be a snap for you. Based upon your list in #3, you will have a pretty good idea of how you wish to proceed with this list. You might decide to talk with a family member, or go through a scrapbook, or do something you've always wished to do even though it gives you the shivers.

*My **hand** moves through my **heart**,*

*gathering the **clouds** of old choices,*

*to **reveal** the light of a **new life***

*ready to be **lived**.*

Appendix

Resources for your next steps.

I f you are looking to take further steps, then you will find a variety of audio downloads, DVDs, classes, programs, and more information about upcoming seminars and other books and publications on Laura's website: www.Laura-Hansen.com

"Hand Me a Wrench" Companion Audio Series

This audio series expands upon the concepts and themes presented in each chapter of the book. Laura led these classes with eight to ten people from around the country gathered to discuss their experiences, questions, and insights of their experience of reading the Wrench book. In each class, the students learn more about how their lives work, and how to create change simply and quickly in their daily lives.

"The Calm at the Center of Your Life: A Life Mechanics™ Workshop" Part 1

DVD with workbook

Be a part of this fun, inspiring, and life-changing workshop. Filmed before a live audience, this workshop offers new perspectives about how your life works, engaging hands-on exercises, and simple action steps for making decisions that support your vision for yourself.

Part 1 offers Laura's introduction to her Life Mechanics method, followed by two interactive exercises: one that helps you find a position of strength within the context of your whole life, and a second exercise that focuses on your relationships and self-image. Complete the exercises along with the attendees, using the same worksheets provided in the seminar.

"The Calm at the Center of Your Life: A Life Mechanics™ Workshop" Part 2

DVD with workbook

The fun, and surprising, insights continue with Part 2. Featuring several spontaneous mini-sessions on stage around the topics of money and career, Laura leads you and the audience through exercises to see your relationship to your work and your money in a new, empowering way.

By the end of the program, you'll have supportive, realistic action steps for three of the most important areas of your life: love, work, and money. Complete the exercises along with the attendees, using the same worksheets provided in the seminar.

Free "Daily Insight" Email/Text Subscription

The Daily Insight gets you thinking about your life in new ways; offers insight into your relationships, goals, and wellness; and provides action steps and exercises for making profound changes in simple ways. Laura wrote these from her explorations as a teacher and guide.

Some Daily Insights are reminders of your capability to create your life according to your vision. Others are simple, fun, experiential energy activities (feeling your own energy centers, talking and listening to plants, magically making your food taste better, etc.). And, some Daily Insights invite you to explore a little more deeply how you create your life, set goals, and express emotions.

Free Online Audio Class MP3s

Since August 2008, Laura has been teaching a free hour-long online class. The tele-class brings people from all over the country together to address a wide variety of topics. In each class, students learn new tools for addressing love, money, career, relationships, health, happiness, and many other aspects of their lives. To join Laura for this class, visit her website for a registration link: www.Laura-Hansen.com

Free Online Article Archive

World hunger, the foreclosure crisis, love, obesity, global politics… no topic is off-limits. Discussing the spiritual mechanics that shape these conditions is the intent for these articles. Entertaining, thought provoking, and compassionate, these insights will leave you nodding your head as you think, "You know… I KNEW that was going on."

Acknowledgements

There are many people in my life I'd like to thank for their support while I wrote this book. First, my husband, Eric, for his loving, inspiring support, much appreciated counsel, and humor every step of the way. And for him finally saying, "Just write how you talk." To my sister, Linda, who read every draft with the same passion and focus with which she lives her life. She was indeed my best editor. To Josie Talamantez and Sandy Harra, two dear friends and fellow counselors who helped me shape the vision of this book and many others now in development. To Lynne Webb and Christy Carrico, for their friendship and support over the months of writing and editing. To Kay Robinson, who was my goals counselor throughout the formation of this book. She was the fixed point on the horizon, like a lighthouse, with whom I found my bearings in the sometimes rough seas of my creative process. To Wendy Newman, my friend and creative co-conspirator who prodded me, saying, "Write this book FIRST! You can write all the others later." She is always right. To my book producer, Brookes Nohlgren, who by asking the right questions helped me write the book I envisioned. And, to the many other friends and colleagues who reviewed various drafts along the way; each offered valuable insight that made this a better book.

About the Author

For over 20 years, Laura Hansen's work has inspired tens of thousands of people through teaching, seminars, private coaching, and speaking engagements. Laura is a public advocate for personal and global wellness. She collaborates with and promotes the good works of champions in such fields as quantum physics, military veteran care, mind/body medicine, human rights, mental health, community activism, and interfaith.

Her methodology, called "Life Mechanics," transforms the conventional psychological treatment model by integrating into it noetic field manipulation and active awareness of the eternal self. This approach helps people work through their problems with exercises – games for adults – that absorb, stimulate, and heal.

Laura holds five spiritual teaching and leadership certifications and four advanced spiritual study certifications, and is an expert in Spiritual Archeology and the Mechanics of Consciousness. She is currently pursuing her Ph.D. in Integrative Studies.

In the early 1990s, Laura ran her own advertising communication company, followed by a product design/manufacturing company for which she holds five design and utility patents as well as awards for its product designs. She also has B.A. degrees in Political Philosophy and English from University of California, Davis.

She lives in Northern California with her husband, Eric, where she paints, designs furniture and clothing, and tries not to kill too many plants in the garden.

More about Life Mechanics and Its Principles

To assist people in understanding how their everyday lives work, Laura Hansen developed Life Mechanics over her 20 years as a spiritual mechanics teacher. Her approach offers a perspective of life that is full of hope, strength, and joy – and every tool and technique has been validated through years of real-life use and client feedback.

This training program includes curriculum levels from beginner to instructor – from one-day workshops, multiple-week classes, to one- and two-year programs, and more. Life Mechanics engages the individual in his or her own world of thought and emotion in a refreshing, understandable way. An individual learns how to use his or her free will to not only resolve experience-based and emotion-based habits, but to access the strength and creativity that naturally reside within.

Life Mechanics Principles

- Consciousness of the individual is by nature stronger than any thought or experience.

- The individual has the power of choice.

- The physical life does not have to be the lone responsibility of the individual. The individual can share it with the consciousness of the universe and the planet.

- Lighthearted exploration and playfulness expands consciousness faster than other mental and emotional states – but all are valid.

- The natural frequency/vibration of the soul is experienced as love.

- The soul experiences itself by interacting consciously with the physical world.

- A soul can choose to experience any part of life or expression.

- A soul is an individual aspect of the universal consciousness.

- An individual's perception and experience of their physical world is an expression of their consciousness.

- Each soul moves along a path of increased consciousness at its own rate – there is no expectation or standard.

Life Mechanics is a continually evolving practice. As you explore your own life with this approach, your point of view and your experience will transform the tools to fit your creative style.

If you are excited to be a more active, powerful influence in your own life, visit the Life Mechanics website: www.Laura-Hansen.com.

(Continued from front of book)

"Laura uses her amusement, compassion, and keen insight into the human experience to show you how, out of the many paths you could travel down this lifetime, to choose one that gives you your heart's desire… And succeed… And have fun learning about yourself and others along the way. Her enthusiasm for showing you the HOW part of achieving your life goals is infectious. Take the time to read this book and practice the exercises; you will be happy you did and amazed at what you discover about your own power, creativity, and possibilities."

Rt. Rev. Christy Carrico
Founder, Ohia Healing Center

"Laura Hansen is a sensitive, brilliant spiritual leader with a deep understanding of the power of spiritual awareness. Her multi-dimensional teaching style has you laughing, stimulates your creative juices, and gives you the safety to let go. Most importantly, she equips you with the nuts and bolts of personal and spiritual enrichment."

Mary Jo See
Author, Natural Genius Books

"Laura Hansen's style is truly unique and incredibly empowering. She has an uncanny ability to listen at the deepest level and understand exactly what is required for your next steps of spiritual growth. I got incredible results in a very short time, and know that her wisdom and gifts can bring anyone to a totally new level of development. I feel blessed to have met such a wonderful mentor and guide to help me on my journey."

Fiona Fay
Human Edge

"*Hand Me a Wrench* is one of the most brilliantly simple and non-judgmental ways I have read for understanding the mechanics of life choices. Laura offers readers an opportunity to see their lives in a non-threatening way, allowing for self-forgiveness, awareness, and action. As one of her long-time students and now fellow spiritual teacher, I find *Hand Me a Wrench* ever relevant, as her wisdom has, for me, facilitated a fresh understanding of my own tools and choices."

Rev. Zenaida Lopez-Cid
Artist

"Laura Hansen has that unique combination of insight, vision, and humor, while being firmly grounded in reality. She is one of the best teachers I have had the pleasure of learning from and she inspires many with her capable leadership qualities in all arenas of her life. This book has the ease of a dear friend encouraging you to fulfill your potential and purpose with practical steps that make it simple and easy."

Ellen Draper
Santa Rosa, CA

"Reverend Laura Hansen is truly blessed on many levels. Grace and beauty define her. Amusement and kindness are her methods of communication. Laura helped me begin shining from the core that is the real me. I now also feel a closeness to God never experienced before in this lifetime."

Rev. Dawn L.
Windermere, Florida

"Laura's calming energy is contagious. The sense of humor she brings to her work is the best! Her style is easy, relaxed, and very, very effective. I always leave one of her classes with a feeling of relief and joy."

Mary Kay Bowar
St. Cloud, MN

"For over 20 years I've watched Laura hone her coaching and counseling skills to assist others to achieve their goals. She is masterful in her ability to pinpoint the crux of an issue, and with gentle humor and simplicity guide her student toward the desired result."

Marcia Kasabach
Bishop, Church of Divine Man

"Laura Hansen has written this book with her signature humor and compassion. She gently reveals to us our ability to reclaim our own soul by realizing that we can make choices that will reflect our true person, and she makes it fun."

Ellie Gregorek
Lincoln, CA

"I have known Laura as my teacher for about five years. In that time her many workshops and counselings have helped me grow as a human being and shine as a spirit. She knows exactly what she's talking about and helps break life down into manageable bits. Besides lots of laughter, she brings wisdom and power that help even the weariest to see their path."

Marion Henshaw
Sacramento, CA

"Laura Hansen is an expert on energetic hygiene. For the same reason we shower and brush our teeth daily – because staying clean doesn't last – we must brush ourselves off energetically each day as well. The tools and techniques Laura offers produce immediate results. Her metaphorical style of delivery is innovative, playful, and provocative."

Cyndi Silva
Founder, Metaphysical Wisdom

"Clarity, down-to-earth goodness, and too-true humor are the hallmarks of Laura Hansen's fun and effective methods of self-healing. Her insights are applicable to all lifestyles, economic conditions, and attitudes. She's a welcome breath of fresh air in any setting. Her work is always valuable to me no matter what mood I'm in! Awesomely enjoyable."

Brianna Lea Pruett
Sacramento, CA

"Your approach to helping me unearth and change old patterns is new and refreshing. Thanks for creating the map – I've already found the treasure!"

Chris Beebe
Partner, www.theVisionaryAgency.com

"*Hand Me a Wrench* encompasses the spiritual practices that allow us to become the creator of our own reality. Laura Hansen introduces simple techniques to set the energy of your life at joy, growth, and happiness. This manual works for the veteran of the spiritual path as well as the novice."

Sandy Harra
Cazadero, CA

"Laura is an absolute inspiration! She possesses an unwavering focus and vision of the truth combined with a hilarious dry sense of humor and engaging personality. Her classes are the safest, clearest, most grounded, and effective by magnitudes. When I think of what a truly brilliant and powerful woman is, I think of Laura – she rocks!"

Lisa Araquistain
www.ClarityforYou.com

"It has been a joy to work with someone who makes the process of enlightenment and growth so fun and insightful. Laura shows up with her loving heart and wants you to be all you can be. If your intent is to find your life's purpose, Laura Hansen can get you there. Take it from me, someone who has been on the journey to find truth my whole life."

Frank Sacco
Film Producer

"Working with Laura is rather like having your own personal lightbulb in the middle of your head that you can turn on when you need an answer. It allows you to see the truth, to get an insight or a revelation when you feel stuck or as though something is missing in your life purpose. Laura's smooth and fine-tuned guidance reconnects your inspiration and purpose with your heart and mind, so that once again you feel completely right with yourself and know exactly what to do next."

Ashleigh B.
Foundation Director

"As a person, Laura Hansen somehow manages to be at once powerful, magnetic, and transformative and simultaneously loving and accessible. Her book promises to be the same."

Sara S. Nichols, RScP
Public Interest Lawyer

Also coming soon from Laura Hansen...

Note to Self: Insights and Affirmations for Living Life Your Way

Available in ebook and paperback. Full-color cover, 4″ x 4″ format. Perfect for tucking away in your bag, or setting on your nightstand.

Preview Excerpt:

Introduction

Since 2007, I've been writing greetings of inner peace – "Daily Insights" is the official name – as a free daily email subscription through my website.

After the first few months, subscribers started asking if I would put together a book of their favorites that they could refer to. To prepare, I asked several die-hard Daily Insight enthusiasts to help me select 150 from the over 400 messages.

How You Can Use the "Daily Insights"

These insights are thought provoking, restorative, and affirming. As a whole, they offer a healthy perspective on how to be an advocate for your own truth and your own life.

Some insights are reminders of your capability to create your life according to your vision, while other passages invite you to explore a little deeper how you create your life, set goals, and express emotions.

I've written these from my own understanding of our spiritual lives. I wouldn't ask you to do or explore something I haven't done myself many times before.

As you use this book, I invite you to allow your intuition and your wonderfully sensitive hands to guide you to the page that has the message with the insight you are looking for.

Sample of Daily Insights included in the book:

Romance can be a ritual of acknowledging the beauty and value of another.

Whom do you value? Who brings beauty into your life?

Stop a moment and consider your life without them. Unthinkable?

Then, celebrate the giver. Celebrate the giving. Celebrate that you can receive such gifts.

———

What moment you live in is up to you.

You can live in a past joy or pain. You can live in a future fantasy.

It's all okay.

Just remember that only in the present moment can you create your life. When you are ready, that moment will be right there with you – ready.

———

God meets us where we are. God doesn't wait until we become better people to talk to us. So, why should we wait until we become better people to listen?

———

Happiness is always appropriate.

———

Is your body having fun? Or are you dragging it around on a leash behind you?

Ask your body what it would like to do today. Promise to give it at least five minutes of whatever it wishes.

Remember, your body can go on strike – not take you where you wish to go, or do what you wish to do.

The relationship between you and your body is an equal partnership. You may forget this, but your body never does...

Don't make it remind you!

———————

Today, make progress on melting the wall between you and someone in your life.

Even if you feel like you are holding a lighter to an iceberg, the gesture will not go unnoticed.

———————

Being happy is way more fun than being perfect. Look for where in your life you are not having fun, and I bet you will find an expectation for you to be perfect.

I bet you a dollar.

———————

When it comes to acceptance, not much has changed since we were kids.

We all still want people to clap when we finish our made-up song, admire our mud pies, and come to our birthday parties.

Today, look for opportunities to express your acceptance of the "kids" around you.

www.Laura-Hansen.com